MW00737955

JOURNEY INTO PRAYER

Gladys,

Blessings, peace
and joy in your
journey.

Carol S. Wolf
3-20-06

JOURNEY INTO PRAYER

Carol S. Wolf

VANTAGE PRESS
New York

The following abbreviations are used throughout this work:

AV   Authorized (King James) Version
NASB   New American Standard Bible
NEB   New English Bible
NIV   New International Version
NRSV   New Revised Standard Version
RSV   Revised Standard Version
TLB   The Living Bible

Illustrated by Dennis King

FIRST EDITION

Published by Vantage Press, Inc.
516 West 34th Street, New York, New York 10001

Manufactured in the United States of America
ISBN: 0-533-11073-4

Library of Congress Catalog Card No.: 94-90097

0 9 8 7 6 5 4 3 2 1

To each person along my journey who has touched my life and taught me something.

To the American Baptist Assembly at Green Lake, Wisconsin, for providing an incredible environment to nurture the soul.

To Carolyn Jennings, my best friend and companion on my journey.

And especially to Dick, my husband, who loves me.

Contents

1. Beginning the Journey   1
2. Glimpses of God's Goodness   5
3. Prayers for Others   21
4. Praying through Scriptures   41
5. Listening to God: Meditation   57
6. Prayer Insights   77

Bibliography   95

JOURNEY INTO PRAYER

1

Beginning the Journey

As a child, I knew three prayers. We said the grace prayer at holidays when Aunt Betty, Uncle Delby, and my cousin Joan came for dinner.

> God is good.
> God is great.
> Thank you for this food.
>   Amen

I loved it when Aunt Betty said her own blessing; it was always a much longer prayer, and it really sounded like she was talking to Jesus.

The second was the nighttime (bedtime) prayer.

> Now I lay me down to sleep,
> I pray the Lord my soul to keep.
> If I should die before I wake,
> I pray the Lord my soul to take.

Then would follow, "God bless Mom and Dad, my sisters and brother, and all my friends." I might even ask to make Jimmy well. He was always having an asthma attack. Or ask for a new bike or to make me thin. I hated my brother calling me "Carol the barrel."

The third was the church prayer (the Lord's Prayer). I said it every Sunday in church, and sometimes I even said it at home after my bedtime prayer. I remember taking it very seriously. It was the perfect prayer that Jesus taught his disciples.

Our Father who art in heaven
Hallowed be thy name
Thy kingdom come, thy will be done,
On earth as it is in heaven.
Give us this day our daily bread
And forgive us our debts,
As we forgive our debtors.
Lead us not into temptation
But deliver us from evil.
For thine is the kingdom,
And the power, and the glory forever.
Amen

Occasionally I was requested to say a sentence prayer at church or Sunday school; then my heart would really pound and skip a beat. Even though I'd manage, I was glad when it was over.

When I was twenty-eight, I discovered a deeper meaning of prayer. My sons were five and eight. Kenneth, the five-year-old, had several unsuccessful kidney operations in three years. He was scheduled for an ileostomy in two days. He'd wear a plastic bag for the rest of his life. My husband, Dick, and I felt helpless. That night we prayed for strength. That same evening a high-school girlfriend, whose husband was doing his residency at a hospital in Boston, called. I poured out our dilemma. Jack got on the phone and said he'd make a few phone calls. The next day he called us. He had made an appointment for Kenny with a distinguished pediatric urologist. We withdrew our consent for surgery, took him out of Children's Hospital of Buffalo, and flew to Boston. After examining Kenny, reviewing the X rays and medical records, the doctor was confident he could repair Kenny's kidneys completely.

Two weeks later, Kenny underwent an eight-hour operation. I felt Jesus with me the whole time. There was a presence surrounding me that entire six weeks. I realized it didn't even matter what the outcome of the surgery was with so much support from our friends, our church, and our family. With God's help, I could handle whatever happened. I discovered prayer from the heart and soul. I experienced what the psalmist said in Psalm 16:11: "You show me the path of life. In your presence there is fullness of joy" (NRSV).

Over the years I have searched, probed, explored, and delved into developing that personal, passionate relationship with God that we read about. Keeping a journal has been especially helpful to me. Rev. Edward Farrell says in his book, *Prayer Is a Hunger:*[1] "Little attention has been given to the value of writing as a way into prayer, an openness to contemplation, as a celebration and remembering, as discovery, as centering."

This is a journal for your prayer journey. It is an opportunity to develop your relationship with God—a chance to enjoy God's company. I have kept a personal record of the experiences in my life, of my relationships, my feelings about events and happenings, and my response to things. It has helped in my search to find out who I am and what is the meaning of my life. A journal is an opportunity to document the greatest of life's adventures—the discovery of yourself.

1. Rev. Edward J. Farrell, *Prayer Is a Hunger* (Denville, N.J.: Dimension Books, 1972), 25.

2

Glimpses of God's Goodness

In Leslie Brandt's version of *Psalms/Now*[1] we read in reference to Psalm 95: "Let us begin this day with singing. Whether we feel like it or not, let us make glad sounds and force our tongues to articulate words of thanksgiving and praise." Yet sometimes it seems much easier to complain and bemoan our situation and to dwell on what we think has gone wrong. Even when God seems silent in our lives, our hearts can be stirred by remembering tiny signs of God's presence and love. I would like to invite you, as you start your journey into prayer, to set aside five minutes every day to recall those moments in the past twenty-four hours that have brought you pleasure. Remember them and relive the enjoyable feelings they brought you. Then record them in this section. Whether it was a bird singing, a smile from a stranger, the sun shining, a parking space close to the door of the grocery store on a rainy day, or a compliment from a friend.

After two weeks of rain and another gloomy day, I wrote: "The flowers look wonderful, the driver who let me merge ahead of him, a phone call from C. and a letter from H." I might have taken all those things for granted had I not spent time reflecting on them.

For most of us, it's easier to focus on the negative happenings. We all have our share of dreary or burdensome days, but these reflections will make a big difference in your

1. Leslie F. Brandt, Psalms/Now (St. Louis: Concordia Publishing House, 1973), 151.

daily attitude. Your five minutes may be found early in the morning, on a coffee break, during lunch or whenever it is convenient for you. What matters is that we come regularly into God's presence with praise. I think that once you start you will look forward to this time each day.

Beginning the Day

I got up early one morning and rushed right
    into the day;
I had so much to accomplish that I didn't
    have time to pray.

Problems just tumbled about me,
    and heavier came each task.
"Why doesn't God help me?" I wondered.
    He answered, "You didn't ask."

I wanted to see joy and beauty,
    but the day toiled on, gray and bleak;
I wondered why God didn't show me.
    He said, "But you didn't seek."

I tried to come into God's presence;
    I tried all my keys at the lock.
God gently and lovingly chided,
    "My child, you didn't knock."

I woke up early this morning
    and paused before entering the day;
I had so much to accomplish
    that I had to take time to pray.
                                    (Author unknown)

I will call to mind the deeds of the Lord; I will remember your wonders of old. I will meditate on all your work, and muse on your mighty deeds.
—Psalm 77:11, 12 (NRSV)

Date:

Every good gift and every perfect gift is from above . . .
—James 1:17a (AV)

Date:

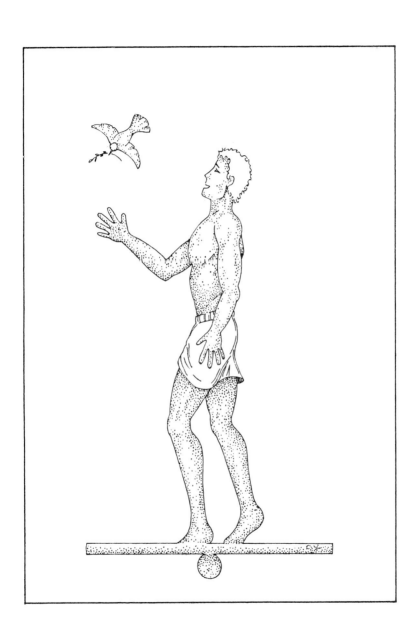

Prayer tomorrow begins today or there will be no prayer tomorrow.

—Edward Farrell
Prayer Is a Hunger

Date:

Relationship with God is what we seek to deepen . . .
—Paul Chaffee
Spirit Awakening: A Book of Practices

Date:

Always be joyful. Always keep on praying. No matter what happens, always be thankful.
—1 Thessalonians 5:16, 17, 18a (TLB)

Date:

Prayer does not change God, but changes the one who prays.

—Soren Kierkegaard

Date:

Say "Thank you" to the Lord for being so good, for always being so loving and kind.

—Psalm 107:1

Date:

It is not enough that we pray outwardly only with the mouth; true prayer, the best prayer takes place in the inner person, and either breaks out verbally or remains hidden in the soul.

—Philip Jacob Spencer

Date:

O sing to the Lord a new song, for he has done marvelous things.

—Psalm 98:1a (NRSV)

Date:

Let your mind drift over the day, attending to and relishing only those moments of the day for which you are grateful.

—Gerard Hughes, SF
God of Surprises

Date:

My heart is overflowing with a beautiful thought!
—Psalm 45:1 (TLB)

Date:

Let there be more joy and laughter in your living.
—Ellen Caddy
God Spoke to Me

Date:

3

Prayers for Others

While praying for ourselves is and should be an active part of our prayer life, praying for others is an important purpose of our being. Jesus spent much of his time in prayer for the disciples and others. He repeatedly told his disciples, "If you believe, it will be so."

Perhaps people pray infrequently because of the question, Does prayer really accomplish anything?

Paul made a practice of praying for his friends. He began several of his epistles by telling them that he thanked God regularly for them and their love for God and for their faithfulness. He was quick to acknowledge how he appreciated them. Paul prayed specifically for difficulties in the churches.

Learning to pray more specifically requires getting to know more about the person or situation. This section enables you to record your specific prayer requests and note when they were received. Our God showers us with so many blessings. If my requests have not been answered, rereading them has given me the opportunity to think about what I have asked for. Do I need to learn patience? For me the answer is a resounding YES! Do I need to remember that all things come in God's right and perfect time, Definitely!

On any trip there is a destination. Our destination is a deeper personal relationship with our Lord. On any trip the more we know about the people, the history, and the situations, the more we get out of it.

One of my favorite stories in Scripture is Jesus' meeting and conversation with the woman at the well. I call her Rachel. In that short encounter, he learned much about her.

She knew the history of the well; she'd had five husbands and now was living with another man. She was religious and was waiting for the Messiah.

Jesus told her who he was, and she believed him. She was anxious to let all her townspeople know. The story in the Scripture ends here, but her life story didn't. There must have been many struggles for her, and we can be sure Jesus kept her in his prayers. Over and over he told the disciples, "Whatever you ask for in prayer, believe that you have received it, and it will be yours."

On the next pages, try praying for a different person or situation each day of the week. Record the person, date, situation, and request. Then for the next week, several weeks or month, pray daily for those listed. Record any answers and date.

This is a wonderful way to see the wonders of God through prayer.

Ask, and you will be given what you ask for.
—Matthew 7:7a (TLB)

	Date	**Request**

Pray
 each day
 for:

Sunday—

Monday—

Tuesday—

Wednesday—

Thursday—

Friday—

Saturday—

No one is insignificant in God's eyes.

Date/Happening:

You should love your neighbor as yourself.
—Matthew 19:19b (NASB)

	Date	**Request**

Pray
  each day
    for:

Sunday—

Monday—

Tuesday—

Wednesday—

Thursday—

Friday—

Saturday—

The secret to enjoying life is to be thankful for what each day brings.

—unknown

Date/Happening:

Dear friends, let us practice loving each other, for love comes from God and those who are loving and kind show that they are the children of God.

—1 John 4:7a (TLB)

	Date	**Request**
Pray each day for:		
Sunday—		
Monday—		
Tuesday—		
Wednesday—		
Thursday—		
Friday—		
Saturday—		

Stick with love . . . hate is too great a burden to bear.
—Martin Luther King, Jr.

Date/Happening:

Do not be anxious about anything, but in everything, by prayer and petition, with thanksgiving, present your requests to God.

—Philippians 4:6 (NIV)

	Date	**Request**
Pray each day for:		
Sunday—		
Monday—		
Tuesday—		
Wednesday—		
Thursday—		
Friday—		
Saturday—		

Troubles are often the tools by which God fashions us for better things.

Date/Happening:

. . . Pray for each other so that you may be healed. The prayer of a righteous man is powerful and effective.
—James 5:15 (NIV)

Date   **Request**

Pray
  each day
    for:

Sunday—

Monday—

Tuesday—

Wednesday—

Thursday—

Friday—

Saturday—

Do not forget prayer. Every time you pray, if your prayer is sincere, there will be new feeling and new meaning in it, which will give you fresh courage.

—Fyodor Dostoyevski

Date/Happening:

Bear one another's burdens.

Galatians 6:2 (RSV)

	Date	**Request**

Pray
  each day
    for:

Sunday—

Monday—

Tuesday—

Wednesday—

Thursday—

Friday—

Saturday—

Oh, what peace we often forfeit
Oh, what needless pain we bear
All because we do not carry
Everything to God in prayer.
                    —Joseph M. Scriven
                        "What a Friend We Have in Jesus"

Date/Happening:

Each morning I will look to you in heaven and lay my requests before you, praying earnestly.
—Psalm 5:3 (TLB)

	Date	Request
Pray each day for:		
Sunday—		
Monday—		
Tuesday—		
Wednesday—		
Thursday—		
Friday—		
Saturday—		

What can one person do? Who can tell, in God's calculations?

—Dorothy Steere

Date/Happening:

I have never stopped thanking God for you. I pray for you constantly.

—Ephesians 1:16 (TLB)

	Date	**Request**

Pray
  each day
   for:

Sunday—

Monday—

Tuesday—

Wednesday—

Thursday—

Friday—

Saturday—

Let us now look specifically at others to discover ways to pray more meaningfully for them.

—William J. Krutza
Prayer—the Vital Link

Date/Happening:

4

Praying through Scriptures

Most of us learn that prayer is talking to God. Many of us do not learn how to listen to what God has to say to us in response. It took me forty years to really, consciously, try to listen. Praying through Scriptures is a means of letting the Gospels or other books in the Bible talk to us today, right where we are at this moment. As we journey on this path, we must believe that the Holy Spirit is alive and well and able to work in our lives.

How does praying through Scriptures work? First, you'll need fifteen to twenty minutes of quiet time and a quiet place. This isn't always easy to find in our busy, noisy lives. You may need to be creative or put a "Do Not Disturb" sign on your door.

The second step is to choose a few verses of Scripture selected to fit your mood and need. You may want to follow through a whole book of the Bible or separate stories. It is helpful to bring whatever historical/cultural understanding of that particular Scripture with you. I have used Haley's *Handbook* for an overview of whatever Scriptures I am using. It is brief and easy to understand. The purpose here is not to recreate the most accurate biblical scene, but instead to allow the story to come alive.

Third, find a comfortable position for yourself. Sitting at a table, in a chair, kneeling, whatever feels comfortable and relaxed. Take time to settle down.

Fourth, begin by reminding yourself of God's presence in your life. Jesus told his disciples, "Believe Me when I say that I am in the Father and the Father in me" (John 14:11a NEB). Likewise, he also continued " . . . you will know that I

41

am in my Father, and you in Me and I in you" (John 14:20 NEB).

Allow yourself to let that presence become real. Try to feel it. Take your time; don't rush. This in itself is prayer. Enjoy the feeling of His Presence, savor it. You may want to acknowledge it with a simple phrase like "Thank you, God" or "My Lord and God" or whatever is meaningful to you. If you don't feel that presence, continue anyway. It may take practice. It took me ages before I felt a difference.

Fifth, read through the passage of Scripture very slowly. Reading it out loud or whispering it helps to remain focused. Pause between phrases; let your mind absorb the words. If a word or phrase seems to be significant, ponder on it. This is prayer, so you don't need to reach any conclusions or resolutions. You don't need to figure out what is meant by every verse. Just let God speak to your soul. Be content with communing with God in this manner.

Try to visualize the setting; then choose one of the characters and let yourself enter into that person's story. Try to hear the sounds, smell the aromas, and feel the emotions. When you have lived out the story, think back to what you have experienced. Were there any new insights or understandings? Did some thought come to mind about your own situation? Thank God for this opportunity to open to God's grace.

The first time I was introduced to this form of prayer, I asked, "How will I know what to think about, and if I imagine the story, how will I know what's right?" I was told that the Holy Spirit works through our thoughts and imagination. I didn't quite believe that until I began to experience it.

This form of prayer is also adaptable to hymns. Try using a hymn book occasionally.

Breathe through the heats of our desire.
Thy coolness and thy balm.
Let sense be dumb, let flesh retire;
Speak through the earthquake, wind, and fire,
O still small voice of calm!

—John Greenleaf Whittier

Date/Scripture/Reflection:

Be still, and know that I am God!

—Psalm 46:10 (NRSV)

Date/Scripture/Reflection:

I will listen, wide awake, to every prayer made in this place.

—Chronicles 7:15 (TLB)

Date/Scripture/Reflection:

Immense hidden powers seem to lurk in the unconscious depths of even the most common man—indeed, of all the people without exception.

—Fritz Kunkel

Date/Scripture/Reflection:

Don't be weary in prayer; keep at it; watch for God's
answers, and remember to be thankful when they come.
—Colossians 4:2 (TLB)

Date/Scripture/Reflection:

The greater the perfection you aspire to have, the more dependent you must become upon divine grace.
—Frank Laubach
Practicing His Presence (Brother Lawrence)

Date/Scripture/Reflection:

O God, nothing that is truly good and worthwhile is withheld from those who walk within your will.
Psalm 84:11b (*Psalms Now*)

Date/Scripture/Reflection:

Even those who have been praying for a while can greatly profit from looking at "old ground" with a fresh eye.

—Michael Francis Pennock
The Ways of Prayer

Date/Scripture/Reflection:

When you pray, go away by yourself, all alone, and shut the door.

—Matthew 6:6a (TLB)

Date/Scripture/Reflection:

Reach high! The best is always kept upon life's topmost shelves, But not beyond our reach if we will reach beyond ourselves.

—Helen Lowrie Marshall
Moments of Awareness

Date/Scripture/Reflection:

5

Listening to God: Meditation

This has been the hardest section to write. I'm not sure why. Maybe because it took me awhile to learn to meditate, but that wasn't the hard part. Listening to God was, and still is, a real tough one for me. It's not that I don't want to listen; I guess I'd prefer that God say what I want to hear.

The two books I used and found most helpful were *Spirit Awakening: A Book of Practices* by Chaffee, Favor, Moremen, Oliver and Wuellner and *Christian Meditation* by Avery Brooke.[1]

Avery Brooke starts her book with this statement: "Meditation, when understood as listening prayer, is our primary means of getting to know God."

Begin any meditation by giving yourself permission to take the time to do the exercise. Formulate a situation or problem in your mind that you would like to ask for guidance about.

Choose a physically comfortable position—a somewhat straight-backed chair so you can breathe free and be relaxed. Allow time for awareness, both bodily and emotional. It is helpful to think of energy or light shining and relaxing through each part of your body. From the bottom of your feet, slowly up to the top of your head, shift your attention to your emotional feelings. Do you have thoughts of anger, anxiety, restlessness, or boredom? Speak to God of those feelings. Don't pretend they aren't there. Invite each feeling to share

1. Avery Brooke, *Learning and Teaching Christian Meditation* (Cambridge: Crowley Publications, 1990), 15.

in your meditation for healing. Then ask all those busy thoughts to step aside for a little while and let you listen.

Relax for a few minutes and be receptive to any feelings, images, or thoughts that come into your mind. Sometimes guidance comes right away. Other times it may come within the next few hours, days, or weeks.

Think of this as a learning process. We aren't a typist the first day in class, nor could we be a surgeon on our first day, week, or month in medical school. It takes time and discipline to achieve communion with God and an awareness of this presence.

It took me a long time of consistent practice before I could even quiet my mind. When I first started to meditate, a hundred different thoughts bounced in and out of my mind with another hundred things I could be doing, should be doing, or needed to do. With perseverance, I got my conscious mind to step aside and let silence settle in. Now I'm hooked! Start with ten minutes and work up. There are many books on Christian meditation for either meditating alone or in a group.

Use this section for recording those thoughts and images, no matter what they are, whether they make sense or not. Then reread and think about them over the next week. It's incredible how many times they have meaning. Just like the song says, "Open my eyes, that I may see. Glimpses of truth, thou hast for me." It took a while to convince me. BUT BELIEVE ME, IT WORKS!

Have no fear of moving into the unknown. Simply step out fearlessly knowing that I am with you; All is very, very well.

Do this in complete faith and confidence.
     —Eileen Caddy
      Footprints on the Path

Date/Ponderings:

But his delight is in the law of the Lord, And on his law he meditates day and night.

—Psalm 1:2 (RSV)

Date/Ponderings:

May my meditation be pleasing to him, for I rejoice in the Lord.

—Psalm 104:34 (RSV)

Date/Ponderings:

There is little sense in attempting to change external conditions; you must first change inner beliefs, then outer conditions will change accordingly.

—Brian Adams
How to Succeed

Date/Ponderings:

One day Jesus told his disciples a story to illustrate their need for constant prayer and to show them that they must keep praying until the answer comes.

—Luke 18:1 (TLB)

Date/Ponderings:

Do not be desirous of things done quickly. Do not look at small advantages. Desire to have things done quickly prevents their being done thoroughly. Looking at small advantages prevents great affairs from being accomplished.

—Confucius

Date/Ponderings:

One day after my return to Jerusalem, while I was praying in the Temple, I fell into a trance.
—Acts 22:17 (TLB)

Date/Ponderings:

Be at Peace and see a clear pattern running through your lives. Nothing is by chance.

—Eileen Caddy

Date/Ponderings:

Sing a new song to the Lord.

—Psalm 96:1a (TLB)

Date/Ponderings:

Learn to be silent. Let your quiet mind listen and absorb.
—Pythagoras

Date/Ponderings:

And when you stand praying, if you have a grievance against anyone, forgive him.

—Mark 11:25a (NEB)

Date/Ponderings:

It is better to wait until we can be honest with God than to rush into praying knowing what we say isn't fully true.

—William J. Krutza
Prayer—The Vital Link

Date/Ponderings:

Now hear my prayers; oh, listen to my cry.
—Psalm 88:2 (TLB)

Date/Ponderings:

True conversation, of course, requires listening as well as talking. We need silent moments of listening if we are to "hear" God speaking to us.

—Michael Francis Pennock
The Ways of Prayer

Date/Ponderings:

6

Prayer Insights

I'm more inclined to call this section "gut feelings." How many times do we get a "gut" feeling to say or do something and frequently do nothing. Then afterwards we say to ourselves "I should have. . . ." I believe "gut" feelings are the Holy Spirit's way of prodding us to care for one another. Wonderful things can happen if you act upon them.

A few years ago, my friend Carolyn and I were at a conference at the American Baptist Conference Center in Green Lake, Wisconsin. Twenty-six of us got together for our first session on Sunday evening. We were introduced to our program leader from South Dakota. Lloyd and his wife, Lena Van Dixhorn, were staying in the same house we were, so after that session, we spent the rest of the evening talking and getting acquainted.

The next morning we learned that Lloyd had been rushed to the hospital during the night and was quite ill. As the day unfolded, we found out he had a malignant kidney tumor and would return to South Dakota within the next day or so. That evening Carolyn and I planned to go out with a few people. Lena returned from the hospital as we were walking out the door. Our "gut" feeling was to ask her if she'd like company for the evening; then we speculated that perhaps she'd prefer to be alone. We did respond to our first feeling and asked her to share our evening. She said yes. Just then Jan DeWitt, the program director, stopped by to see how Lena was doing. She invited the three of us to her home for tea. That evening we felt God's presence.

Two weeks later, I received a note from Lena. Here are a few comments I will cherish forever: "I will never forget the support I felt that night in Jan's sunroom. I was so weak and you women were my strength. . . . I thanked my heavenly Father for a sister like you. I hope we meet again. . . . Lloyd is doing great. . . . The doctor was so very happy because he expected the worst . . . My love and thanks."

Think about a time you wanted to give someone a word of encouragement or touch their hand and say "I understand" but felt reluctant to do so. Next time you feel those urges, say or do exactly what you feel inspired to do. You will be pleasantly surprised.

We've lost track of the model Jesus set for us when he began his public ministry. He reached out and touched all types of people from all walks of life. He did it spontaneously and with love.

Many years ago Carolyn gave me a candle. It says: "God touches us through our friends."

This part of your book is a place for recording your prayer insights or "gut" feelings. A place to prompt you to action. A place to record the proddings of the Spirit and your response. Be it a card, a letter, a phone call, or a word of encouragement, this is a place to record those promptings and then to look back and remember the joyful responses.

You can refine your intuition by learning to listen to your inner feelings and acting upon them. Acting upon those urges may be a leap of faith and trust. Think back to the times you have listened to your inner feelings, acted upon them, and then were amazed at what happened.

It does require flexibility and spontaneity. To develop those qualities takes being willing to sometimes let go of your plans and go where the Spirit leads. There have been times when I have felt "out on a limb." It gets easier every time, and I have no regrets.

I've enjoyed sharing this journey with you. I'm getting used to those curves in the road that cause my path to change directions. I hope you do too. My prayer for you is to keep an open mind, to explore, and to experience all that life has to offer. God loves each of us and wants to be our friend and companion.

Dare to Be Happy

Dare to be happy—don't shy away,
Reach out and capture the joy of today!

Life is for living! Give it a try;
Open your heart to that sun in the sky.

Dare to be loving, and trusting, and true;
Treasure the hours with those dear to you.

Dare to be kind—it's more fun than you know;
Give joy to others, and watch your own grow.

Dare to admit all your blessings, and then
Every day count them all over again.

Dare to be happy, don't be afraid—
This is the day which the Lord hath made!
                              (Author unknown)

Treasure your journal as I have mine. Blessings, peace, and joy in your travels.

I must explore, and search until I find the rest of me;
when I possess my soul, then—then will I be whole.
                                        —Helen Lowrie Marshall
                                        A Gift So Rare

Date/Insight/Promptings:

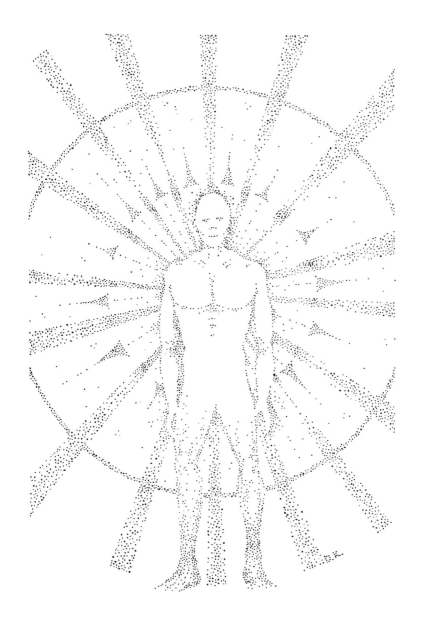

A time to keep silence and a time to speak.
—Ecclesiastes 3:7b (NRSV)

Date/Insight/Promptings:

There is no greater blessing than a friend who's there when the good times aren't.

—unknown

Date/Insight/Promptings:

Why am I praying like this? Because I know you will answer me, O God! Yes, listen as I pray.
—Psalm 17:6 (TLB)

Date/Insight/Promptings:

Lord, teach us to pray.

—Luke 11:1b (NEB)

Date/Insight/Promptings:

Settle yourself in solitude and you will come upon Him in yourself.

—Teresa of Avila

Date/Insight/Promptings:

Man cannot discover new oceans unless he has courage to lose sight of the shore.

—Andre Gide

Date/Insight/Promptings:

Pray that I will be bold enough to tell it freely and fully.
—Colossians 4:4a (TLB)

Date/Insight/Promptings:

We need to find God, and He cannot be found in noise and restlessness. God is the friend of silence.

—Mother Teresa

Date/Insight/Promptings:

. . . the Holy Spirit helps us with our daily problems and in our praying.

—Romans 8:26a (TLB)

Date/Insight/Promptings:

One word of cheer that we may say, could carry farflung consequence, and might make all the difference.
—Helen Lowrie Marshall
Moments of Awareness

Date/Insight/Promptings:

Bibliography

Brandt, Leslie F. *Psalms/Now*. St. Louis: Concordia Publishing House, 1973.

Brooke, Avery. *Learning & Teaching Christian Meditation*. Cambridge: Crowley Publications, 1990.

Chaffee, Paul et al. *Spirit Awakening: A Book of Practices*. San Francisco: Word Press, 1988.

Farrell, Rev. Edward J. *Prayer Is a Hunger*. Denville, New Jersey: Dimension Books, 1972.

Krutza, William J. *Prayer—The Vital Link*. Valley Forge, Pennsylvania: Judson Press, 1983.

Laubach, Frank. *Practicing His Presence*. Auburn, Maine: Christian Books, 1973.

Marshall, Helen Lowrie. *A Gift So Rare*. Kansas City, Missouri: Hallmark Cards, 1969.

Marshall, Helen Lowrie. *Moments of Awareness*. Kansas City, Missouri: Hallmark Cards, 1968.

Pennock, Michael Francis. *The Ways of Prayer: An Introduction*. Notre Dame, Indiana: Ava Maria Press, 1987.